runtherace

LIFETOUCH SERIES

Walking in the Spirit: A Study Through Galatians 5
Run the Race: A Study Through Hebrews 12

runtherace

A STUDY THROUGH

HEBREWS 12

STEVE PETTIT

journeyforth®

Greenville, South Carolina

All Scripture is quoted from the King James Version.

The fact that materials produced by other publishers may be referred to in this volume does not constitute an endorsement of the content or theological position of materials produced by such publishers.

Photo Credits: Steve Pettit ©2014, Hal Cook, BJU Photo Services; iStockphoto.com © aarrows (silhouette of runner)

Run the Race: A Study Through Hebrews 12
Steve Pettit

Contributor: Eric Newton
Designer: Elly Kalagayan
Page layout: Michael Boone

© 2015 by BJU Press
Greenville, South Carolina 29614
JourneyForth Books is a division of BJU Press

Printed in the United States of America

ISBN 978-1-60682-977-6

15 14 13 12 11 10 9 8 7 6 5 4 3 2 1

I dedicate this book to the memory of my friend, Tom Craig,
who finished his earthly race
and entered into his reward of eternal rest
on September 3, 2014.

He shepherded his flock with character and compassion
and preached God's Word with clarity and conviction.

We will remember his life and follow his faith.

CONTENTS

1 INTRODUCTION   1

2 RUN THE RACE   11

3 LOOKING UNTO JESUS   22

4 WE NEED ENDURANCE   32

5 THE CHASTENING OF GOD'S CHILDREN   41

6 THE LOGIC OF SUBMISSION   52

7 THE WAY OF RENEWAL   61

8 FINAL WARNINGS   70

(1)

Introduction

The Message of Hebrews:
An Antidote for Spiritual Apathy

....

Reading Hebrews is like reading a powerful sermon (Heb. 13:22), though it traveled in the first century as a letter. Experts consider it "the most extensively developed and logically sustained piece of theological argumentation in the whole of the New Testament."[1] There is no mention of the author's name, but he demonstrates an extraordinary grasp of the Greek language and an impressive writing style. And he wastes no time in introducing his subject. We find the grand theme of Hebrews in the opening paragraph (1:1–4): *After speaking in various ways at various times, God has revealed Himself supremely and savingly through His Son, Jesus Christ.*

Q: *Note the descriptions of Jesus Christ in Hebrews 1:2–4. Summarize them in your own words.*

---

[1]Philip E. Hughes, *A Commentary on the Epistle to the Hebrews* (Grand Rapids: Eerdmans, 1977), 35.

_____

_____

_____

_____

Q: *How do these descriptions of Christ contribute to your understanding of what Hebrews is all about?*

_____

_____

_____

_____

This unknown author wrote from an unknown location to an unknown group of believers. Because the author mentions Italy (13:24), most scholars believe Hebrews was written to a house church in Rome. These Jewish believers had heard the preaching of the apostles (2:3–4), but they had never seen Jesus. They had been faithful to God in the past in spite of enduring suffering, hardships, and persecution from the Roman government (10:32–34). This persecution may have come in AD 49 during the reign of Claudius when he expelled the Jews from Rome (Acts 18:2).

The immediate circumstances that serve as the backdrop of this letter happened nearly fifteen years after the previous persecution. Current believers had yet to face martyrdom (Acts 12:4), but with Nero as emperor the prospect of violent persecution loomed ominously before them. Fearful about what could happen to them because of their faith, they were beginning to slip spiritually (Heb. 2:1). Some were tempted to return to Judaism, while others had withdrawn from public worship (10:25). The prevailing danger was that these Christians would become slack and fall away from their faith in Christ. Public outcry against and humiliation of Christians would escalate once again. For Jewish believers, reverting to a former paradigm (Old Covenant) seemed the logical way to ease the abuse by fellow Jews and remove the onus of social alienation.

Q: *What factors in today's world put pressure on Christians to shrink back from publicly identifying with Christ?*

_____

_____

_____

_____

_____

In contrast to this false solution, Hebrews teaches us how to respond to circumstances that challenge our faith. God had spoken to the Jewish people throughout their history at many different times and in many different ways. He communicated through the prophets with multiple promises concerning the coming Messiah. Now, these promises had been fulfilled in time ("these last days") through the coming of God's Son, Jesus Christ. His prophetic word is the final and ultimate revelation of God.

The book of Hebrews unfolds in a two-beat rhythm. The author presents theological explanations of the person and work of Jesus Christ followed by practical exhortations to be faithful to God. He presents the excellence and supremacy of Christ and the New Covenant by contrasting them with various aspects of the Old Covenant such as angels, Moses, the Levitical priesthood, and animal sacrifices. In the end, it is very clear that Jesus Christ with His New Covenant is so much better than what the Jews had under the Old Covenant.

You can greatly enhance your study of Hebrews 12 by reading through the entire book of Hebrews first, even if you do so quickly.

Q: *List the references in Hebrews where you notice words such as* **better, superior, excellent,** *and* **perfect.**

_____

_____

_____

_____

_____

This exposition of Christ's greatness carries a definite *wow factor*. We cannot help but be impressed with who Jesus is and what He has done as the author carries us to lofty theological heights. However, portions of the exhortation convey a *woe factor*. The rewarding end of faith is powerfully contrasted with the cursed outcome of unbelief. The logic for us to consider is clear: if the unbelieving and disobedient Israelites suffered severely for their apostasy (i.e., claiming to know God but not continuing in faith), how much greater will be the judgment on those who fall away from their professed belief in Jesus Christ?

Our privileges as Christians today are so much greater than what God's people experienced under the Old Testament system. Those saints possessed promises that were never fulfilled within their lifetimes. What they longed to see was not consummated until the coming of Jesus Christ and the establishment of the New Covenant. We are presently living in the last days, the time of fulfillment of God's Word and promises. Today, everything is better! Therefore, we have all the more reason to be faithful to God.

But saying everything is better is not the same as saying everything is easy. Whether you are a first-century Christian in Rome or a twenty-first-century Christian in America, there is significant pressure to grow apathetic in your walk with Christ and even to turn away from the faith you once professed. Christian schools and Bible-preaching churches are full of second- and third-generation "Christians" who assume a one-time decision for Christ guarantees heaven. The writer of Hebrews, like James, teaches that true faith endures and bears fruit. Salvation is by faith in Christ alone, but that faith presses on and goes the distance. Only by persevering in the Faith will we realize the goal of eternal salvation. The author of Hebrews commands us to persevere in our faith through a powerful metaphor—run the race!

Q: *What are some specific temptations that second- and third-generation Christians face?*

Q: *What have you learned from this introduction to Hebrews that can strengthen Christians facing these pressures?*

The Hall of Faith: A Prelude to Hebrews 12

There is one more stop we need to make on our way to the starting line of Hebrews 12. Its first verse begins with the word *wherefore*. The passage we are studying is intentionally attached to the preceding context, sometimes called the Hall of Faith. So before starting our trek through Hebrews 12, we should note three key aspects of the chapter before it—Hebrews 11.

First, notice the recurring theme of faith. Forms of this word occur twenty-fives times in the forty verses in this chapter. The author uses these men and women as examples because they placed their confidence in God. The point of these examples, however, is not merely that they had an internal trust in God. The point is that they *lived* by faith. Abel offered a sacrifice by faith (11:4). Enoch pleased God by faith (11:5). Noah constructed an ark by faith (11:7). Abraham searched for the Promised Land by faith (11:8) and offered up Isaac by faith (11:17). Sarah was able at ninety years old to bear a son by faith (11:11). And so the chapter goes. Saying we believe is one thing, but those who run successfully actually do more than assent to the truth. They *live* by faith.

Take some time to underline or highlight all the references to faith in Hebrews 11. Notice the names included among faithful saints. Some were great (Abraham), some were unlikely (Rahab), many were inconsistent (Gideon, Samson, Jephthah), and most went unnamed (e.g., those who suffered mocking and imprisonment).

Q: *If neither pedigree nor perfect performance unifies the examples in Hebrews 11, what does?*

_____

_____

_____

_____

_____

Q: *Why do you think God works this way?*

_____

_____

_____

_____

_____

Second, take a moment to identify the object of these saints' faith. Sometimes faith can be viewed as blind optimism or even naïveté. But it is very clear in Hebrews 11 that the faith of our Old Testament predecessors had *content*. They trusted in God and, specifically, in what He had said. Abel evidently responded to God's directions about sacrifices (11:4). Noah responded to God's warning about a flood (11:7). Abraham responded to God's call to leave Ur (11:8). Abraham's son Isaac and grandson Jacob similarly acted on the basis of God's promise (11:9).

Q: *What other indications do you find in Hebrews 11 that the content of faith is what God has said?*

_____

_____

_____

_____

_____

Anyone can try to be hopeful about the future—perhaps because of technology or medicine or family prominence or seeming financial success. But the only source of true hope is our covenant-keeping God. We can be faithful because He is faithful.

Q: *What implications does this aspect of Hebrews 11 have for how you read and value God's word?*

_____

_____

_____

_____

_____

Q: *How should this testimony to the importance of God's Word affect your view of pleasing God?*

_____

_____

_____

_____

_____

A third observation about Hebrews 11 is for us to note God's response. God's people respond to God's Word *in faith*, and God responds to His people's faith *with reward*. Notice what Hebrews 10:35 says. The author exhorts his readers not to throw away their confidence because it carries a great (literally, *mega*) reward. He goes on to say that faith is the instrument through which Old Testament saints received commendation ("a good report," 11:2). This theme emerges in 11:4–6 as well. (Note also what 11:26 says about Moses.) Our God is not a slave-driver. He doesn't demand blind loyalty. Though we could never earn His favor, He is pleased when we live by faith. He rewards those who diligently seek Him (11:6). He has given us more than enough motivation to run this race!

Q: *Since these believers did not receive what was promised (Heb. 11:39), how was their faith rewarded (e.g., Abraham; Gen. 15:1)?*

_____

_____

_____

_____

_____

Q: *Is the reward that motivated the Old Testament saints (Heb. 11:16, 20, 26) an incentive for us today, or should we be pursuing "some better thing" (Heb. 11:40)?*

_____

_____

_____

_____

_____

Discussion Questions

1. *What is the relationship between what these people believed and how they lived?*

_____

_____

_____

_____

_____

2. How would you summarize the theme of Hebrews 11?

_____

_____

_____

_____

_____

3. Was the way of faith different for Old Testament believers than it is for New Testament Christians? If not, what does this have to do with your life in the twenty-first century?

_____

_____

_____

_____

_____

2

Run the Race

HEBREWS 12:1
*Wherefore seeing we also are compassed about with so
great a cloud of witnesses, let us lay aside every weight, and
the sin which doth so easily beset us, and let us run with
patience the race that is set before us.*

The Christian life of faith is descriptively called a race.
Hebrews 11 surveys Old Testament saints for illustrations
of imperfect men and women who took God at His Word and
lived accordingly. At the beginning of Hebrews 12, the author
turns his attention to us. He begins with a challenging exhortation to join the likes of Abraham, Moses, and Joseph and run
this race.

Picturing Our Motivation to Run

HEBREWS 12:1
Wherefore seeing we also are compassed about
with so great a cloud of witnesses, . . .

WORD STUDY

wherefore—then; for which reason; consequently

compassed—to lie around; to be encircled; surrounded

so great—of a quantity; so many

cloud—a large dense multitude, a throng; used to denote a great shapeless collection of clouds obscuring the heavens as opposed to masses of clouds with some form or shape

witnesses—those who provide evidence or share legal testimony; in a historical sense, those who are spectators of something

The challenge to run the race begins with a motivational metaphor. A great host of people have assembled to bear testimony to the faithfulness of God and to provide evidence that finishing the race is indeed attainable. The term *witnesses* refers to the catalog of faithful Old Testament men and women described in Hebrews chapter 11 whose lives testified to their faith.

Q: *Choose one key figure from Hebrews 11, and describe some aspects of his or her journey of faith.*

_____

_____

_____

_____

There are so many of these witnesses that they are described as "so great a cloud." Don't imagine a single, cumulus cloud perched in a sky of blue, but rather the entire visible sky blanketed with a dense cloud covering. This great crowd is like an ancient stadium filled to capacity. It isn't so much that these witnesses are looking at us from heaven but rather that we are looking to them for encouragement. These are no ordinary spectators but people who have successfully run the race before us.

Q: *Why should we be encouraged by the testimony of these Old Testament believers? In what ways can you identify with them?*

_____

_____

_____

_____

_____

This inspirational motivation is based on a comparison between Old Testament saints and believers today. Look at how Hebrews 11 begins: "Now faith is the substance of things hoped for, the evidence of things not seen. For by it the elders obtained a good report" (11:1–2). And this is how it ends: "And these all, having obtained a good report through faith, received not the promise: God having provided some better thing for us, that they without us should not be made perfect" (11:39–40). The writer announces that these men and women had received divine approval because of their loyalty to God and their enduring faith.

This commendation would be significant on its own, but it is even more remarkable because they never saw God's promises fulfilled in their lifetimes: "These all died in faith" (11:13). Let this sink in. These Old Testament saints believed in the glorious promises of God, set their hopes upon them, and endured faithfully through hardship and suffering; however, they lived and died "and received not the promise" (11:39). The unfulfilled promise is described as being "made perfect" (11:40). In fact, we get our term *martyr* from the Greek word translated *witnesses*.[1] Not all of these Old Testament believers were martyrs, but some were. And even when facing death for their faith, they

_____

[1]Origen, an early church leader (AD 250), defines a martyr as "one who of his own free choice chooses to die the for the sake of religion." Quoted in Jack Mulder, *Kierkegaard and the Catholic Tradition* (Bloomington: Indiana University Press, 2010), 236 n45.

persevered though they had "received not the promise." It's as if these Old Testament saints successfully finished the race without ever having seen the finish line.

Before Christ, the Jews were limited in their relationship with God. Access into His presence was strictly prohibited (9:8). God-ordained sacrifices abounded, but freedom from a guilty conscience was virtually unknown (9:9). Consequently, the advent of Christ changed everything. His coming inaugurated a new and better day: "God having provided some better thing for us" (11:40). God plans to perfect us through the sacrifice and ministry of Jesus Christ (10:14). We now have unrestricted access to God so we can enjoy His presence with a conscience cleansed from sin. The author's exhortation is clear: since we enjoy greater privileges, how much more faithfully should we live in comparison to the witnesses of Hebrews 11?

Q: *Reflect on the superior privileges we have as beneficiaries of the New Covenant. List other privileges we now have. What should these advantages prompt you to do?*

Carefully Preparing to Run

HEBREWS 12:1
. . . let us lay aside every weight, and the sin which doth so easily beset us, . . .

WORD STUDY

lay aside—to put off or away

weight—whatever is prominent; bulk, mass; hence, a burden or encumbrance

sin—missing the mark; erring or being mistaken; missing or wandering from the path of uprightness and honor; doing or going wrong

easily beset—skillfully surround or thwart

Have you ever gotten excited about going somewhere only to realize partway through the trip that you didn't adequately prepare? We must respond to God's challenge to run with both willingness and careful preparation. All athletic training requires intense conditioning. Running is agonizing! A runner has to get his body into shape by disciplining himself and laying aside excess weight. The goal of a serious runner is a perfect body weight for maximum performance. Losing weight requires various forms of self-denial, such as cutting out unnecessary amounts of food. In the ancient games, runners would even remove all their clothes before the race began. This assured them that nothing would impede their freedom while running. In our lives, weights are not necessarily unlawful aspects of life. They are simply hindrances to living by faith.

Take a look at 1 Corinthians 6:12, where Paul refers to the question of lawfulness. He then proceeds to raise two additional concerns that are crucial for determining how to please God in our everyday lives.

Q: *What are Paul's two concerns? Write down at least one example of a lawful behavior that you should probably still forgo. Why is this choice important?*

_____

_____

_____

_____

_____

We are constantly surrounded by multiple distractions that can lead us away from a passionate following of Christ into a state of unbelief—living for the temporal benefits and pleasures of this present world. (See 2 Tim. 4:10.) These encumbrances demand both our time and energy and diminish our commitment to spiritual growth and service to God. We must decisively "lay them aside."

Q: _According to 2 Timothy 4:10, why did Demas leave Paul? If Demas were alive today, what attractive elements of this present world might draw out his love and weigh him down?_

_____

_____

_____

_____

_____

Q: _What is weighing you down? What hindrances are impeding your spiritual progress?_

_____

_____

_____

_____

Besetting sins are often individual in nature and peculiar to one's personality. The potential effect of these sins on us is devastating. The book of Hebrews has five major warning passages concerning the disaster of falling into sin and leaving one's faith (apostasy) for this present evil world. Look at what these warning passages teach us.

- **Hebrews 2:1–4**—Paying close attention to God's revelation of Jesus Christ is crucial to our faith.

- **Hebrews 3:12–4:11**—We cannot realize eternal "rest" without exhorting one another daily to turn away from sin and believing what God has said.

- **Hebrews 5:11–6:8**—Disinterest in God's Word evidences spiritual immaturity, and neglecting basic biblical doctrine is the road to falling away from the Faith.

- **Hebrews 10:32–39**—Disregarding what Christ has accomplished on the cross provokes divine judgment, and enduring faith is necessary to receive what God has promised.

- **Hebrews 12:25–29**—Those to whom the New Covenant has been revealed must not refuse to listen to the God of heaven, who is a consuming fire.

Q: *What about these warning passages caught your attention? Why?*

Q: *Since we cannot lose our salvation (e.g., John 6:37; 10:29), what purpose do these warnings serve?*

_____

_____

_____

_____

Q: *What besetting temptations or sins do you need to seek God's grace to lay aside?*

_____

_____

_____

_____

Responding to a Powerful Exhortation to Run

HEBREWS 12:1

. . . and let us run with patience the race that is set before us, . . .

WORD STUDY

run—exert oneself, as runners in a race; to strive hard; spend one's strength in performing or attaining something. This verb can refer to incurring extreme peril, which requires the exertion of all one's effort to overcome.

patience—steadfastness; constancy; endurance; perseverance. The term is used in the New Testament as the characteristic of a person who is not swayed from his deliberate purpose or his loyalty to faith and piety by even the greatest trials and sufferings.

race—the place of contest; the arena or stadium; the

competition for a prize; generally, any struggle or contest

set before—placed in front of a person; before the eyes; in sight; standing forth; appointed, destined

The challenge to run the race concludes with a powerful exhortation. The Greek word for race is *agon*. An *agon* was a stadium or an arena where intense footraces were run. This word connotes a great contest like the Olympics or a heroic struggle like a battle. This image of a contest describes our entire life as Christians. All of us begin the *agon*—the race—at the point of personal confession of faith in Jesus Christ.

Q: *Read Luke 13:24. What does this verse communicate about our entering into a life of faith in Christ?*

_____

_____

_____

_____

_____

Q: *What does the word* patience *indicate about the race of life? Read Hebrews 10:23. What is one of our primary motivations for persevering in faith?*

_____

_____

_____

_____

This race continues as we pursue holiness and strive for Christlikeness. Paul uses this term *agon* in Colossians 1:29 and 2:1 to describe himself and, by extension, all those who aggressively minister the gospel through evangelism, church planting, and discipleship. Though each one of us commences the race in the same way, it is the Master of the race who determines the exact course that each runner will follow. We must faithfully run this race throughout our lives. It is not completed until every runner enters into heaven in an eternal, glorified state.

Q: *The author says this race is "set before us." Why is this significant? What does this tell you about God's intentions for your life? (Notice the similar wording about Jesus in Heb. 12:2.)*

_____

_____

_____

_____

_____

Q: *Read 1 Corinthians 9:24–27. List the ways you should be running the race.*

_____

_____

_____

_____

_____

Victory is not determined by who crosses the finish line first but simply by who finishes the race. The issue is not speed but stamina. We need to patiently and persistently stay the course. By finishing, we confirm the authenticity of our saving faith. Therefore, run the race!

Q: *According to 2 Timothy 4:6–7, how do you know if you have won this race?*

_____

_____

_____

_____

Discussion Questions

Q: *Is it beneficial to look back at the spiritual journeys of other believers who have run before us? Why or why not? If so, what could you do to learn from others?*

_____

_____

_____

_____

Q: *If the writer of Hebrews was writing to believers, and if all believers are running the race of the Christian life, then why did he need to exhort us to run? Why is this significant for your own life's marathon?*

_____

_____

_____

_____

3

Looking Unto Jesus

HEBREWS 12:2
Looking unto Jesus the author and finisher of our faith;
who for the joy that was set before him endured the cross,
despising the shame, and is set down at the right hand of
the throne of God.

If you've done much running, you know how important inspiration is. It's not enough to suit up in designer running clothes and shoes and make sure your keys and wallet aren't weighing down your pockets. Preparing to run in this way is certainly advisable. But if you want to run successfully, you need someone or something that keeps you going.

To run the race of life, we need to lay aside weights and besetting sins and run with endurance, and to do so, we need more than mere human examples. We need an Enabler. We need a Savior. Hebrews 12 clearly describes the means by which this race is to be run. We run by "looking unto Jesus," or to put it more fully, by maintaining a resolute focus on the person and work of Jesus Christ.

Looking to Jesus Christ

HEBREWS 12:2
Looking unto Jesus the author and finisher of our
faith; . . .

WORD STUDY

looking—looking away from all others, looking up to

author—a chief leader, captain, or prince

finisher—a completer

our (or the) faith— faith as a whole from its beginning to its end (as indicated by the definite article preceding the noun in Greek)

The phrase "looking unto Jesus" means "looking away from all else to Jesus." How can we do this, you might ask? **First, we need to avoid distraction.** In the middle of a stormy sea, Jesus commanded Peter to get out of the boat and come to Him by walking on the water. After Peter climbed out of the boat, "he walked on the water to go to Jesus" (Matt. 14:29). As long as he kept his focus on Christ, he was able to continue his miraculous stride of faith. However, when he shifted his attention from the Master to the tempest, he began to sink. Peter fearfully cried out to Jesus to save him. The Lord reached out His mighty hand and rescued the disciple from great danger. Quickly, Jesus admonished him for his unbelief: "O thou of little faith, wherefore didst thou doubt?" (14:31).

Q: *Peter could actually see the Lord. How can you focus on Christ since He isn't physically near you? What verse(s) support your position?*

_____

_____

_____

_____

The key to staying on top of the water is ignoring distractions and keeping our focus on Jesus. Likewise, runners can't get distracted in the life of faith. Can you imagine trying to run a race while looking at the crowds in the stands? What happens to those who take their eyes off the goal and turn around to watch the other runners in the race? They don't win!

Q: *What distracts you from running by faith? (Perhaps these distractions are similar to the weights referred to in Hebrews 12:1.) How can you tell when you are not focusing on Christ? What are the results?*

———————————————

———————————————

———————————————

———————————————

———————————————

Second, we need to concentrate on one person—Jesus Christ. After pointedly preaching to the Jews, Stephen faced the onslaught of an angry, bloodthirsty crowd. Acts 7:55 begins the account of his martyrdom. While those in the mob gnashed their teeth at Stephen, he looked into heaven and saw Jesus standing at the right hand of God. In the hour of his death, he gazed resolutely on the exalted Christ, undistracted by what was going on around him (7:56–57). Even in his last moments, he was asking Jesus to receive his spirit and to forgive the attackers (7:58–60).

Q: *What does Stephen's response to his circumstances teach you about looking to Jesus? At what moments are you perhaps most tempted to look to others instead of to Christ?*

———————————————

———————————————

———————————————

———————————————

The author of Hebrews challenges us to keep "looking unto Jesus" as Stephen did. "Such concentrated attention on the person of Jesus and his achievement epitomized the fundamental challenge of Hebrews."[1] We should benefit from the examples of faithful men and women of the past. We should lay aside weights and sins that weigh us down and trip us. But in order to run faithfully to the end, we must fix our gaze on Jesus Christ. He is "the way, the truth, and the life" (John 14:6).

Looking to Jesus Christ's Saving Work

From the very beginning of Hebrews, the writer contrasts Christ with the Old Covenant.

Q: *For example, read Hebrews 8:6–13. Why is the New Covenant superior to the Old Covenant? What are the four promises the Lord makes in 8:10–12 as part of the New Covenant?*

_____

_____

_____

_____

Every element of the Jewish faith was only a shadow when compared to the person of Jesus Christ. Everything He accomplished was so much better! He was the complete and final revelation of God's truth to the world; He fulfilled all the

---

[1]David Peterson, *Hebrews and Perfection* (Cambridge: Cambridge University Press, 1982), 170.

promises spoken by the prophets to the forefathers; He gave Himself as the perfect sacrifice for sins; He was exalted at the right hand of the Father; He replaced the Old Covenant; He perfected believers. Earlier in this epistle the author exhorted believers to look to Christ in faith: "consider the Apostle and High Priest of our profession, Christ Jesus" (Heb. 3:1). Now, the command is to run the race by "looking unto Jesus, the author and finisher of our faith" (12:2).

What does it mean for Jesus to be "the author and finisher of our faith"? In terms of what He objectively accomplished for us, this means that Jesus led the way in the life of faith. He ran His own race and was the champion of faith from start to finish. The word *author* is translated in Acts 3:15 as "Prince" and in Hebrews 2:10 as "captain." This term refers to someone who blazes a trail, originates an idea, or leads the way. Jesus "perfected living by faith"[2] and "is the man of faith par excellence."[3]

Q: *What does it mean that Jesus Christ ran His own race? Look up Hebrews 2:10–18. How do these verses help you understand the significance of Christ's own race on earth? How does this encourage you?*

---

[2]R. Kent Hughes, *Hebrews: An Anchor for the Soul* (Wheaton: Crossway, 1993), 2:161.

[3]Philip E. Hughes, *A Commentary on the Epistle to the Hebrews* (Grand Rapids: Eerdmans, 1977), 522.

Christ was also the "perfecter" of our faith by establishing the New Covenant for us. Under the incomplete Old Covenant, no human could ever gain access to God's presence. Now, under the Christ-initiated New Covenant, all believers have a "perfect" relationship with God. This relationship includes unlimited access to God's presence, a conscience washed clean by the blood of Christ through His once-for-all sacrifice (Heb. 10:14), and a new heart regenerated by the Holy Spirit.

In terms of what Christ personally applies to us, this means He is the one who initiates and bestows faith within the believer's heart. (See Phil. 1:29.) This divine enabling of faith is also, according to Philippians 1:6, the guarantee and confidence that God will bring to a successful conclusion our life of faith. Therefore, throughout the entire race we must constantly look to Jesus as "the author and finisher" of our life of faith.

Looking to Jesus Christ's Example

HEBREWS 12:2

. . . who for the joy that was set before him endured the cross, despising the shame, and is set down at the right hand of the throne of God.

WORD STUDY

joy—delight

set before—set forth or exhibited

for—usually means instead of (substitution); here it means in contrast with (distinction)

endured—stayed behind; bore with patience

despising—thinking little of; looking down on

set down—made to sit down; appointed

right hand—a position of authority

Sometimes well-meaning people emphasize Jesus' example to such a degree that Christianity is reduced to the question *What would Jesus do?* That isn't a bad question. But by itself it misses the huge point that Christ doesn't merely show us the way. He also paid for our ability to travel that way by His righteous life and atoning death. In other words, we look to Him as "the author and finisher of our faith." But the verse doesn't stop there. We also look to Him as the example of how to persevere in trusting the Father. *What **did** Jesus do?* is a very good question. So, what does His example entail?

First, Jesus endured by focusing on the eternal prospect of joy. This was the joy referenced in Psalm 16:11, a joy Jesus knew He would receive when He entered into His Father's presence in heaven. This joy would come as a result of finishing His eternal work of redemption by suffering on the cross and by being exalted to His Father's right hand of power. This was the joy that Jesus would experience by "bringing many sons unto glory" (Heb. 2:10; cf. Luke 15:7). This promise of joy lodged in the forefront of His mind.

Q: *Can there be a difference between happiness and joy? If so, what would distinguish them? Are there indications in your life that you are living for mere happiness and not everlasting joy?*

_____

_____

_____

_____

_____

Q: *What aspects of the person and work of Jesus Christ cause you to rejoice? What do they have to do with the trials and temptations you may be facing?*

_____

_____

_____

_____

_____

Second, Jesus endured by keeping the ultimate benefit of His suffering before His mind. The world viewed the cross as a place of abject shame. Death by crucifixion, as one of the cruelest forms of execution, was reserved for only the worst criminals. Jesus held the world's view of the cross in contempt. According to 1 Corinthians 1:23–24, instead of the cross being an object of shame, it manifested the wisdom and power of God. It was at the cross that God reconciled the world to Himself. It was at the cross that God's wrath was fully exhausted. It was at the cross that God magnificently displayed His love for the world. It was at the cross that God could be both just and the Justifier of those who believe in Jesus. Therefore, Jesus viewed everything about the cross differently. He disregarded the shame of the cross and treated it as if it were nothing compared to what God would gloriously accomplish through His suffering and shame.

Q: *How does the cross display God's wisdom and power? Meditate on 1 Corinthians 1:23–31. How does this put the cross in perspective for you? How does this differ from the perspective of the unbelieving world?*

_____

_____

_____

_____

_____

"Looking unto Jesus" is the primary means by which we run the race of faith. "Looking unto Jesus" is sufficient for living the Christian life. No believer will ever fail by "looking unto Jesus."

Discussion Questions

1. *Can you think of other metaphors similar to "author and finisher" that express the scope of what Jesus did for us (e.g., Rev. 1:8)?*

_____

_____

_____

_____

2. *If Jesus is your example, name one thing He did that you could do today or tomorrow.*

_____

_____

_____

_____

3. *What aspect of Jesus' persevering faith most challenges or encourages you? What will you do to meditate on this reality, to keep it in front of you as you seek to run the race of faith this next week?*

_____

_____

_____

_____

_____

4

We Need Endurance

HEBREWS 12:3
For consider him that endured such contradiction of sinners
against himself, lest ye be wearied and faint in your minds.

So far, we have seen that the Christian life means responding to God's call to run, shedding our hindrances, and maintaining a single-minded focus on Jesus Christ. Now that we are off and running, the author challenges us with our need for one thing all long-distance runners find essential—endurance.

Chapter 12 of Hebrews is a continuation of thought that the author began two chapters earlier in 10:32–39, where he references the persecution his original readers had experienced at the hands of the Roman government. Around AD 49, many Jewish Christians were thrown into prison. Suetonius's biography of the Emperor Claudius records that "there were riots in the Jewish quarter at the instigation of Chrestus. As a result, Claudius expelled the Jews from Rome."[1] The belief of most historians is that *Chrestus* is a reference to Christ.

---

[1]Suetonius, quoted in R. Kent Hughes, *Hebrews: An Anchor for the Soul* (Wheaton: Crossway, 1993), 2:19.

Christians had been banished from the synagogues by Jewish leadership. Consequently, these believers experienced mockery, public abuse, imprisonment, shame, the plundering of their property, and hardships. However, during these trials they showed courage and patiently endured with a resolute faith.

At the time Hebrews was written, some fifteen years later, the believers were facing the possibility of a new wave of persecution from the government. Fearful, they were struggling spiritually and were tempted to abandon the Faith they had once confessed for the false refuge of the Old Covenant. Beginning in 10:36, which says, "Ye have need of patience," and continuing through 12:7, the author focuses on their (and our) need for endurance.

> Let us run with patience the race that is set before us . . . (12:1)

> Who for the joy that was set before him endured the cross . . . (12:2)

> For consider him that endured . . . (12:3)

> If ye endure chastening . . . (12:7)

We can best understand this emphasis on endurance, especially Hebrews 12:3, by answering three questions.

What Is Endurance?

Patience, endured, and *endure* in these verses are all forms of the Greek word *hupomeno,* which means "to abide or stay under." Endurance is a firm resolve not to quit. In light of the race metaphor, it means to finish what we start in spite of any difficulty or pain. In relation to faith, it means to maintain our confidence in God regardless of the obstacles and opposition.

One of the reasons we can continue trusting God in the midst of trials is that He ultimately controls them. Hebrews is one of the General Epistles. Two others, James and 1 Peter, also speak to believers who were experiencing adversity. Notice what the following passages say about God's control of and purposes in our trials.

Q: *What does James 1:2–4 say about how faith is tested and proved?*

_____

_____

_____

_____

_____

Q: *What does 1 Peter 1:6–7 say about how faith is tested and proved? What does this passage teach you about God and your trials? How does this passage encourage endurance?*

_____

_____

_____

_____

_____

As we faithfully persevere under trials, resisting the temptation to quit and absorbing the pressure, we will develop endurance in our lives. It's like concrete that settles and hardens over time; faith is solidified as we endure trials. Endurance is crucial because it is God's means of developing in us a settled and solid faith.

Q: *Peter refers to God and suffering again in 1 Peter 5:10. What are the outcomes of enduring such adversity?*

_____

_____

_____

_____

_____

Why Do We Need Endurance?

HEBREWS 12:3

. . . lest ye be wearied and faint in your minds.

Before discussing how we can endure, let's take a closer look at what the original recipients of this letter were facing. The believers in Rome were being persecuted by the Roman government and religious antagonists. These conflicts affected the early Christians both emotionally and spiritually. The author pictures these internal struggles with two verbs that refer to physical fatigue.

WORD STUDY

wearied—worn out, exhausted

faint—to give up, quit, or bail out of something

mind—*psyche*; inner person or soul controlled by the mind

Being wearied means coming to a point where you are sick and tired of something. It's the process of being worn down, losing resolve, and giving up. To faint in your mind is to lose heart. You can't take it any longer, and you want out now! One pastor describes faintness in terms of a person who says, "I'm doing it, and I am done with it!" Aristotle used the same verb to describe the condition of runners who collapsed from exhaustion after crossing the finish line.[2]

The writer of Hebrews wants to encourage us not to falter before crossing the finish line. Some believers in the first century were withdrawing from fellowship while others were drifting back into Judaism. The ultimate threat was that they would become so discouraged that they would walk away from the Faith. We may not be experiencing physical persecution, but it is just as important for us to hold fast to our faith and endure victoriously to the end.

Q: *Have you or someone you know well ever been discouraged about the Faith and tempted to start giving up? Did you or this friend tend to withdraw from God's Word and from fellowship with God's people? What counsel would you now give based on what you are learning from this passage?*

_____

_____

_____

_____

Q: *Read Acts 4:23–31. What situation did the apostles find themselves in? What truths about the Lord did they reaffirm in prayer to Him? What were the results?*

_____

_____

_____

[2]John Sandys, ed., *The Rhetoric of Aristotle* (Cambridge: Cambridge University Press, 1877), 3:93.

What Is the Means of Endurance?

HEBREWS 12:3
For consider him that endured such contradiction
of sinners against himself, . . .

WORD STUDY

for—a conjunction used to express cause, explanation, inference, or continuation

consider—give careful attention to; examine minutely and from all angles; reason with careful deliberation

endured—stayed behind; bore with patience

contradiction—dispute, hostility, rebellion; obstinate and argumentative opposition

sinners—unsaved people who opposed Christ during His life, both Jews and Gentiles

The author has already pointed out that we find the power to keep running by "looking unto Jesus" (Heb. 12:2). Now he gives the imperative: "Consider him that endured such contradiction of sinners." In other words, we should mentally compare Christ's sufferings to ours. He endured more than we ever will. By reflecting on His example in relation to the hostility shown to Him by sinners, we gain strength to bear our trials in a proper manner. Considering Jesus provides us the power and strength to endure.

To "consider him" means to meditate on the passion of Christ, to examine all the details of the sufferings of Jesus. Chrysostom explains the "contradiction of sinners" as "an allusion to the full range of abuses that befell Jesus in his passion."[3] Over and over He faced the hostility of wicked men from every angle. His reputation was constantly maligned, defamed, ridiculed, and slandered. His arrest and subsequent trial violated all the proper procedures of the ancient Jewish judicial system. His death sentence was a Roman political ploy to silence the bloodthirsty cries of the crowd. His scourgings were a public mockery. His crucifixion was the crime of eternity. Yet, throughout the entire passion, Jesus never once yielded to sin! We are urged to turn these events over and over in our minds. Why? Because meditating on Jesus is the only way to face discouragement.

See how He suffers, yet without sin. Watch Him as He agonizes in the Garden of Gethsemane while anticipating the sufferings of the cross. See Him sweating great drops of blood. Observe His meekness as He stands before His accusers like a gentle lamb. Hear the crowd cursing His name and calling for His blood. Be astounded that He never offers one word of defense to His accusers, even when given the opportunity. Feel the blows coming down on His head and back as He is "wounded for our transgressions" and "bruised for our iniquities" (Isa. 53:5) Hear the thud of the wooden mallet as iron spikes are driven into the Savior's hands and feet. Try to fathom the Father forsaking Him. Listen to Him as He makes supplication for His murderers and forgives His offenders. Hear His trust in the Father's good pleasure. The best way to draw strength and encouragement for the race is to reflect on His agony.

Q: *Pick a couple of the truths about Jesus' suffering mentioned above. Meditate on them. Write out the significance of them in your own words.*

---

[3]*Patrologia* 63:195–96, cited by N. C. Croy, *Endurance in Suffering* (Cambridge: Cambridge University Press, 2005), 189.

_____

_____

_____

_____

_____

Being diligent to consider Him is essential to our sanctification. We do not find strength to run the race in self-effort or willpower. We discover and experience spiritual strength by faith through our union with Christ. The entire human life of Christ is ours by faith and is the source of our sanctification. In 2 Corinthians 3:18 we see that as believers gaze into the Word of God, the ministry of the Holy Spirit takes what is Christ's and progressively applies it to us.

- He applies Christ's death to us for the pardon of our sins.

- He makes Christ's endurance through suffering available to us.

- He imparts Christ's power and holiness unto us by faith so that we are able to overcome discouragement and run the race with endurance.

Q: *What enabled Jesus to endure "such contradiction of sinners against himself"?*

_____

_____

_____

_____

_____

Discussion Questions

1. *What is discouraging you right now? How does Christ's suffering put that circumstance in perspective? What can you do to draw strength and encouragement to keep running?*

_____

_____

_____

_____

_____

2. *What does Jesus' holiness have to do with yours (Heb. 12:10; John 17:19)? Restate what you have learned regarding how to grow in holiness by meditating on Christ's sufferings and on what He accomplished through those sufferings.*

_____

_____

_____

_____

_____

5

The Chastening of God's Children

HEBREWS 12:4–8

Ye have not yet resisted unto blood, striving against sin. And ye have forgotten the exhortation which speaketh unto you as unto children, My son, despise not thou the chastening of the Lord, nor faint when thou art rebuked of him: For whom the Lord loveth he chasteneth, and scourgeth every son whom he receiveth. If ye endure chastening, God dealeth with you as with sons; for what son is he whom the father chasteneth not? But if ye be without chastisement, whereof all are partakers, then are ye bastards, and not sons.

If you have ever played sports, you know there are some aspects of the game you can control. Basketball players can run wind sprints, practice free throws, draw up offensive plays, and watch video footage of opponents. But you cannot prepare for everything. The bus may get stuck in traffic and leave little time for warm-up. The opposing team may employ a new defense. Your star player may suffer a random injury.

In the Christian life, we have the responsibility to set aside weights and besetting sins (Heb. 12:1), to look to Jesus Christ (12:2), and to persevere by faith (12:3). But we also face pressure and adversity that is impossible to control or perhaps even anticipate. Living successfully means not only heeding God's instructions but also responding in faith to God's corrective training. That's what these next few verses talk about.

The picture now shifts from a race to a family. Forms of the key words *sons* and *chastening* are each used five times. This section addresses the loving discipline of God's children. The trials and suffering we experience are a part of the Father's training and discipline of us as sons. Like Jesus, the recipients of Hebrews learned "obedience by the things which [they] suffered" (Heb. 5:8). And so do we.

Q: *What are some things in your life that you cannot control? Which of these do you feel are outside of God's control?*

_____

_____

_____

_____

_____

Why Should We Not Grow Weary?

HEBREWS 12: 4–5
Ye have not yet resisted unto blood, striving against sin. And ye have forgotten the exhortation which speaketh unto you as unto children, . . .

WORD STUDY

resisted—set down against; opposed

striving—struggling against (same root word as *race* in Heb. 12:1)

have forgotten—have become utterly oblivious and totally unaware of what is happening

exhortation—a calling to one's aid; referring to the actions of someone who encourages, comforts, and consoles

speaketh—addresses or discusses a subject

These verses extend the thought begun in Hebrews 12:3, namely that believers should consider Him (Christ), who endured the hostility of sinners against Himself. We are in a struggle with our sinful human nature. The picture is of hand-to-hand combat in ancient warfare. But no one in the fight against sin has shed any blood like Christ did on the cross.

Another thing that will keep us from giving up in the battle is focusing on our relationship with God through Christ—we are His children, and that's the way He treats us and talks to us.

Q: *Jesus was tempted in all things just as you are (Heb. 4:15), but how were His experiences of temptation different from yours?*

_____

_____

_____

_____

_____

HEBREWS 12: 5-6

... My son, despise not thou the chastening of the Lord, nor faint when thou art rebuked of him: For whom the Lord loveth he chasteneth, and scourgeth every son whom he receiveth.

WORD STUDY

despise—to consider something to have little value; to feel contempt for

chastening—the rearing of a child; training, discipline

faint—loosened; weakened, released; grew weary, failed

rebuked—exposed, convicted, or reproved

loveth—difficult to define but beautifully described in 1 Corinthians 13:1-8

chasteneth—instructs, disciplines; trains children; corrects

scourgeth—whips or beats with a whip

receiveth—accepts or admits

What Is Chastening?

The word *chastening* ranges in meaning from educating, instructing, and teaching to punishing. It was often used to refer to the process of training children. Chastening is the means by which sons and daughters are disciplined and brought to maturity. Though chastening has negative elements, it is primarily a positive idea. God uses suffering in our lives as an instrument of His chastening.

Q: *Write down an example of how a teacher might chasten students in order to help them learn and grow.*

_____

_____

_____

_____

_____

How Is Chastening a Problem for Believers?

Evidently, the original recipients of this letter were experiencing some forms of persecution or resistance. Because of this adversity, some of them were veering away from the Faith. The author mildly rebukes his readers and charges them with forgetting the wisdom of Proverbs 3:11–12: "My son, despise not the chastening of the Lord; neither be weary of his correction: For whom the Lord loveth he correcteth; even as a father the son in whom he delighteth." They had failed to consider the truth that divine chastening is a clear sign of divine love: "Ye have forgotten the exhortation . . . For whom the Lord loveth he chasteneth" (Heb. 12:5–6). God intends for us to respond to His loving chastening with humility and obedience.

However, when we forget God's love, we tend to react negatively to trials in two ways. First, we despise the trials: "My son, despise not thou the chastening of the Lord" (12:5). In this context *despise* means to regard trials as having little value. We might evidence this disregard through irritation, complaining, questioning, failing to receive them as divine admonitions, not seeing any gracious design and objective purpose behind them, and resenting them with expressions of contempt and scorn. How quickly we're blinded to the value that struggles bring into our lives! Philo, a Hellenistic Jewish philosopher who died around the time Hebrews was probably written, put it this way: "So profitable a thing is some sort of hardship that even its most humiliating form, servitude, is reckoned a great blessing."[1]

Q: *Think of a time in your life when you experienced adversity or correction. How did you respond? What value or purpose could there have been in your God-ordained circumstance?*

_____

_____

_____

_____

Second, we sometimes lose heart in trials; we "faint when [we are] rebuked of him" (12:5). We are not to be overwhelmed or dismayed by our trials. We are not to focus on the difficulty of

---

[1]Philo, quoted in F. F. Bruce, *The Epistle to the Hebrews* (Grand Rapids: Eerdmans, 1990), 343.

the struggle but on our relationship with God. He "scourgeth every son whom he receiveth" (12: 6). The fact that chastening is sent by our loving Father means that trials are worthy of our careful attention and patience.

Q: *Why do you think we so often get discouraged during trials? Have you ever experienced this? What were your thoughts toward God during those times?*

_____

_____

_____

_____

_____

HEBREWS 12:7–8

If ye endure chastening, God dealeth with you as with sons; for what son is he whom the father chasteneth not? But if ye be without chastisement, whereof all are partakers, then are ye bastards, and not sons.

WORD STUDY

if—whether; used in conditions and in indirect questions

endure—stay behind; bear with patience

dealeth—treats; behaves oneself toward someone

for—indeed; used to express cause or provide explanation

without—separately, separate from; apart from

chastisement—instruction, discipline

all—every

partakers—participants; those who share in

bastards—illegitimate children

What Is the Proper Attitude Toward Chastening?

Hebrews unlocks one of the great keys to overcoming discouragement. In D. Martyn Lloyd-Jones's religious classic *Spiritual Depression*, he addresses the way believers handle the mental and emotional struggles of life. His advice is to counsel yourself from the Word of God. You need to talk to yourself in biblical terms instead of merely listening to yourself.[2]

Q: *Why is it necessary to talk to yourself instead of listening to yourself? Have you ever done this? What biblical truth did you meditate on?*

_____

_____

_____

_____

_____

First of all, look back at the first verse of this section. The author of Hebrews reminds us that in our striving—our *agon*, our race—against sin, no one has suffered like Jesus did: "Ye have not yet resisted unto blood, striving against sin" (12:4). Jesus faced great pressure from Satan and an evil world, but He resisted it all the way to the cross instead of losing faith in His Father. In comparison to His sufferings, our struggles are minor. Life is sometimes very difficult, but we need to remind ourselves that our great Savior went the distance and endured the unimaginable to show us the way and to get us there. We

[2]D. Martyn Lloyd-Jones, *Spiritual Depression* (Grand Rapids: Eerdmans, 1965), 116–17.

have to tell ourselves this truth instead of merely listening to our flesh.

Q: *Are you currently going through suffering of some kind? How does your perspective about it change if you think about Jesus' striving to the death against sin?*

_____

_____

_____

_____

_____

Second, chastening is God's process of discipline. Even though Hebrews 12:7 begins with *if*, it's a statement of fact: you *are* enduring chastening. It is also a statement of purpose: you are enduring trials and hardships for the purpose of discipline. The heavenly Father's education program for His children is learning through endurance. Even Christ experienced chastening: "Though he were a Son, yet learned he obedience by the things which he suffered" (Heb. 5:8). Jesus, as the author of salvation, is the ultimate example of the relationship between being a son and suffering.

Q: *Does it seem odd at first that Jesus learned something? Why was this necessary if He is perfect? So what does this mean for you since you are far from perfect?*

_____

_____

_____

Third, God is treating us as a father would treat his own son.
In fact, He is treating us better than any earthly father could
because He is perfect in wisdom, power, and love. Discipline
is clear evidence that we are a child of God: "If ye endure chastening, God dealeth with you as with sons; for what son is he
whom the father chasteneth not?" (12: 7). Do you know of
any good father who doesn't correct and train his children?
He does so because wants the best for them even if they cannot understand. All believers are partakers of God's discipline
because our heavenly Father knows what is best for us even
when we cannot understand.

Q: *Has there been a time in your life when God, perhaps
through a loving human authority, disciplined you? Did
you initially understand what God was doing? What good
came about because of this correction?*

The author is drawing from an Old Testament teaching: "Thou
shalt also consider in thine heart, that, as a man chasteneth
his son, so the Lord thy God chasteneth thee" (Deut. 8:5).
Loving chastening has always been God's method of growing
His children.

**Fourth, if we never undergo discipline, it indicates that
we are not in God's family.** Never experiencing chastening
sounds easy but is actually deadly. Someone who professes

faith in Christ but never experiences divine discipline is an illegitimate child! He is born out of wedlock and is usually abandoned by a father who avoids all responsibility for the provision, instruction, and discipline of the child. Derelict fathers often conceal their identities and remain anonymous. However, God never treats His own children in that manner. He is worthy of His name—Father. God paternally cares for His own children; He gives attention designed to correct our faults, change our behaviors, and benefit us both in this life and in the life to come.

Q: *When was the last time you experienced divine discipline? What was God teaching you about Himself? If this experience happens tomorrow, what truths from this study would you tell yourself in order to respond in faith?*

_____

_____

_____

_____

The ancient words the writer of Hebrews quoted from Proverbs 3:11–12 are intended for our counsel today: God loves me and chastens me for my own benefit. My trials are for my good! They are designed to correct the faults in my life. This is good advice that we need to remind ourselves over and over.

Discussion Questions

1. *Do you as a follower of Christ need to resist "unto blood, striving against sin"? If not, why not? If so, how can you hope to do that?*

_____

_____

_____

_____

_____

2. *John Chrysostom, an early church father who lived around AD 400, said, "It is those very things in which they suppose they have been deserted by God that should make them confident that they have not been deserted by God."*[3] *What do you think he meant by that? Is it a scriptural viewpoint?*

_____

_____

_____

_____

3. *What is the key to unlocking discouragement as presented in Hebrews?*

_____

_____

_____

_____

_____

[3]Chrysostom, quoted in Philip E. Hughes, *A Commentary on the Epistle to the Hebrews* (Grand Rapids: Eerdmans, 1977), 528.

6

The Logic of Submission

HEBREWS 12:9–11

Furthermore we have had fathers of our flesh which corrected us, and we gave them reverence: shall we not much rather be in subjection unto the Father of spirits, and live? For they verily for a few days chastened us after their own pleasure; but he for our profit, that we might be partakers of his holiness. Now no chastening for the present seemeth to be joyous, but grievous: nevertheless afterward it yieldeth the peaceable fruit of righteousness unto them which are exercised thereby.

Have you ever been assigned a difficult task that didn't seem to have a point? It is almost impossible to work up the motivation necessary to fulfill such an obligation. Throughout human history God has called His people to do hard things. Sometimes the point is a mystery, as with Job suffering undeserved pain and loss and Joseph being sold into slavery. At other times the Lord declares the goal. Think of Noah building an ark to preserve his family and the animals. Or Abraham leaving Ur to find the unknown Promised Land. Or Moses going back to Egypt to lead the Israelites out of bondage. When it comes to discipline, God does not merely tell us to submit, though that is His sovereign right; He persuades us with compelling reasons.

We saw in the previous section that a proper response to divine discipline is foundational for the spiritual life of God's children. The author of Hebrews has already made it clear that all of God's sons—even Jesus, His unique, beloved Son—experience chastening through suffering and hardships. The passage continues its focus on the Lord's discipline by helping us understand why God displays His fatherly love this way. Using logic called *a fortiori*—arguing from the lesser to the greater—the author gives us three reasons to submit to our heavenly Father.

Q: *Why do you think God often doesn't give us details about our journey in advance but still assures us of our final destination?*

_____

_____

_____

_____

_____

Submitting to Our Spiritual Father

HEBREWS 12:9
Furthermore we have had fathers of our flesh which corrected us, and we gave them reverence: shall we not much rather be in subjection unto the Father of spirits, and live?

WORD STUDY

furthermore—then, next, therefore (an adverb denoting sequence)

flesh—generally, human beings or the human body, though Paul uses it to describe corrupt human nature; in this case, a description of the fathers who physically procreate us in contrast to God, who is the Father of our spirits

corrected—instructed or disciplined

gave reverence—respected

much rather—to a greater degree

be in subjection—to yield; to place oneself under; to submit to another's control

spirits—wind, breath; human soul

live—to have true spiritual life

The first reason to submit is stated as a question: if we are willing to respect our earthly fathers, then how much more should we subject ourselves to our heavenly Father? Earthly fathers bring children into this world through physical procreation and then discipline them for their own benefit in this present life. All correction, admonition, and even punishment are given with the hope that children will be able to function properly and be well adjusted in life. As a result, children show respect to their fathers through humble obedience.

In contrast, our heavenly Father not only created all human beings but is also the giver of eternal life. Hebrews calls Him "the living God" (3:12; 9:14; 10:31; 12:22) and the one who has opened up a "new and living way" to heaven by the sacrifice of Jesus Christ (10:20). All of God's discipline has a view towards our spiritual benefit in this life and in the life to come. To submit to Him is to experience life "more abundantly" (John 10:10). "Those who live life to the fullest do not buck God's discipline—but rather embrace it."[1]

Q: *The book of Proverbs states that wisdom begins with fearing the Lord and continues with listening to mature, fatherly instruction (Prov. 1:7–8). Although the respect due earthly fathers is not the primary point, what does this passage take for granted concerning our response to parental correction?*

---

[1] R. Kent Hughes, *Hebrews: An Anchor for the Soul* (Wheaton: Crossway, 1993), 2:173.

_____

_____

_____

_____

Q: *Read 2 Corinthians 4:16–18. What does Paul say God is accomplishing through affliction? How do the affliction and the reward compare?*

_____

_____

_____

_____

Submitting to Perfect Discipline

The second reason to submit can also take the form of a question: if our earthly fathers disciplined us with sometimes fallible reasoning, and we submitted to them, then how much more should we obey our heavenly Father whose discipline is always perfect? Most parents look back on the years they were rearing their children and acknowledge many mistakes they made. Sometimes their discipline was too hard and at other times too soft. In some instances they acted wisely, but at other times their responses reflected a spirit of irritation, anger, or moodiness. Their judgment was often swayed by favoritism, prejudice, and ignorance. Yet, in spite of all these faults, children were still required to show respect and to submit to their correction.

Q: *How should you respond to mistakes parents make? What scriptural principles guide you to respond rightly?*

_____

_____

_____

_____

_____

In contrast, God's discipline begins at the moment of our conversion and continues throughout our entire lives. All along
the way, His correction has no faults or errors in either its purpose or its application. Whatever suffering comes our way, we
can rest assured that this is the best, wisest, and most loving
choice. Everything He does in discipline is for our profit—so
that we can be partakers in His holiness. As we gladly submit
to His chastening, we are changed more and more into His
likeness and enjoy more and more of His presence. Our Father
knows and wants what is perfect for our lives!

Q: *Read Psalm 103:8–14. Notice what it says about the
Lord. Take a moment to reflect on the reality that, if you
are a true believer in Christ, God is your perfect, loving Father.
Write out what this has to do with your present circumstances.*

_____

_____

_____

_____

_____

Submitting for Our Eternal Benefit

HEBREWS 12:10–11

For they verily for a few days chastened us after
their own pleasure; but he for our profit, that we
might be partakers of his holiness. Now no chastening for the present seemeth to be joyous, but

grievous: nevertheless afterward it yieldeth the peaceable fruit of righteousness unto them which are exercised thereby.

WORD STUDY

verily—indeed; used to affirm or emphasize

few days—short time

chastened—instructed or disciplined; trained children; corrected

after their own pleasure—according to their own thinking or opinions

profit—to bring together; to be expedient

partakers—ones who share in, receive together

holiness—sanctity

present—currently; at the time

seemeth to be—is considered, is accounted as

joyous—delightful

grievous—causing mental pain; sorrowful

afterward—last, later

yieldeth—gives back, pays; returns, restores, rewards someone with

peaceable—without turmoil

fruit—benefit, produce

righteousness—justice

exercised—trained strenuously

The third reason we should submit comes out of this question: if there is benefit in all earthly discipline, then how much greater is the spiritual benefit for those believers who properly respond to the Father's discipline? Chastening is never considered a joyful experience when a child is under the correction of his parents. It is painful in nearly every possible way—whether it's a spanking, a privilege removed, a possession taken away, an unwanted responsibility, or a verbal reprimand. However, most adults who were properly disciplined as children can look back with gratitude and respect toward their parents. They have learned that there is a positive outcome! Their experiences of discipline molded their lives and enabled them to become what they are. Likewise, no chastening from God is a joyful experience in the moment of pain—sickness, financial loss, distress, persecution, or verbal attacks. However, there is a future reward. God is doing His deepening work in our lives. C. S. Lewis wrote, "God whispers to us in our pleasure, speaks in our conscience, but shouts in our pain: it is his megaphone to rouse a deaf world."[2]

Q: *Why do adversity and failure make you more aware of God's voice? Does this mean you should desire pain? What should you want more than easy circumstances?*

_____

_____

_____

_____

A holy life is of far greater value than the earthly blessings of family, friends, health, or prosperity. As we develop humility, faith, and obedience in the *exercise* (a form of the word from which we get *gymnasium*) of God's discipline, we reap the benefits of suffering: "And the fruit of righteousness is sown in peace of them that make peace" (James 3:18). The peaceable fruit that is produced is confidence in God and quiet trust in

---

[2]C. S. Lewis, *The Problem of Pain* (London: Centenary Press, 1940), 81.

His sovereign control. ". . . In returning and rest shall ye be saved; in quietness and in confidence shall be your strength" (Isa. 30:15). When we accept discipline as something designed for our good, we will stop feeling resentment and rebellion toward God. When we respond in faith to God's discipline, we enjoy a close walk with Him and a life that conforms to His righteous standards. Through gracious logic God compels us to understand that His discipline is for our good.

Q: *Hebrews 12:11 says that God exercises, or strenuously trains, His children to produce practical righteousness. Why is this necessary? Are you experiencing this in your life? If so, how?*

_____

_____

_____

_____

_____

Discussion Questions

1. *What are some ways God disciplines you? Why does He do it? What difference does it make how you respond to discipline?*

_____

_____

_____

_____

2. *Read what Psalm 119:67 and 71 say about about the outcome of affliction. What are some truths about discipline you can learn from these verses?*

_____

_____

_____

_____

_____

3. *What's the connection between the words* discipline *and* discipleship? *How should this affect your life this week?*

_____

_____

_____

_____

_____

7

The Way of Renewal

HEBREWS 12:12−14

Wherefore lift up the hands which hang down, and the feeble knees; And make straight paths for your feet, lest that which is lame be turned out of the way; but let it rather be healed. Follow peace with all men, and holiness, without which no man shall see the Lord.

The writer of Hebrews has just explained why God disciplines His children. Suffering and hardship can easily discourage us and make us feel rejected. Instead, we can accept this discipline, remembering that God loves us as only a perfect Father can. With these truths in mind, the author returns to the image of running the race (12:1–2). He gives three direct commands to those who have been weakened by discouragement and need to get back in the contest. These exhortations instruct us in the way of renewal. We need to resolve, remove, and pursue.

Resolve!

HEBREWS 12:12

Wherefore lift up the hands which hang down, and the feeble knees . . .

WORD STUDY

wherefore—consequently; on account of this

lift up—set straight again; to raise, restore, make straight

hang down—relax; let go, droop

feeble—weakened, disabled; paralyzed or loose

First of all, to be renewed we must resolve! The word *wherefore* at the beginning of this verse connects the outcome of chastening to the necessity for renewal. The Greek word translated "lift up" means to set something straight. From this term we derive our word *orthopedics*, which refers to setting straight or correcting deformed bones or muscles. The Hebrews 12 runner is described as having drooping hands and feeble knees. He is worn out, discouraged, and ready to quit the race. He needs to be restored and reinvigorated with fresh, new strength.

Q: *Has there been a time recently when you have felt worn out? Perhaps you've even contemplated dropping out of the race. What circumstances prompted these feelings and thoughts?*

_____

_____

_____

_____

_____

This image of lifting up hands and knees comes from Isaiah. Even though the nation of Israel would experience defeat and exile, God was encouraging the Jews through Isaiah's prophecy that they would be restored from bondage in a pagan land: "Strengthen ye the weak hands, and confirm the feeble knees. Say to them that are of a fearful heart, Be strong, fear not: behold, your God will come with vengeance, even God with a recompense; he will come and save you" (Isa. 35:3–4).

Earlier in Hebrews, divine intervention had already been assured to those who were in need of persevering faith: "For yet a little while, and he that shall come will come, and will not tarry. Now the just shall live by faith . . ." (Heb. 10:37–38). Those who are righteous in Christ live by faith in God's promise. Christ has come once, and He will come again.

We find strength in the promise of Christ's Second Coming and experience strength as we trust and obey. The strength to get up and run the race is found when we resolve to get up and run the race.

Q: *Read Hebrews 3:15-4:2. Why do you think the unbelieving Israelites mentioned in these verses lacked the resolve to get up and run the race?*

_____

_____

_____

_____

_____

Shortly after Pentecost, Peter and John met a lame man sitting at the entrance gate of the temple in Jerusalem. The poor man begged the disciples for some money, but Peter wanted to give this man something far better! "Silver and gold have I none; but such as I have give I thee" (Acts 3:6). The lame man was offered healing when Peter commanded him: "In the name of Jesus Christ of Nazareth rise up and walk." And he responded in faith to Peter's offer: "He [Peter]took him by the right hand, and lifted him up: and immediately his feet and ankle bones received strength" (Acts 3:7). The lame man was given the strength to stand and the ability to walk when he chose to stand and walk! God imparted supernatural strength *in the act of faith*. Do we desire spiritual renewal? God revives us with His divine power when we resolve to intensely pursue Him.

Q: *Look back at a couple of the examples of faith in Hebrews 11. Remember how those Old Testament believers not only assented to the truth but also acted on it in faith? What truth about God do you need to act on today in the face of difficulty?*

_____

_____

_____

_____

_____

Q: *Read Isaiah 40:28–31. How does Isaiah describe God? What are the effects of God's person and work on those who are weary?*

_____

_____

_____

_____

_____

Remove!

HEBREWS 12:13

And make straight paths for your feet, lest that which is lame be turned out of the way; but let it rather be healed.

WORD STUDY

straight—right, in the sense of firm or smooth

paths—tracks of a wheel; tracks or courses

lest—or else; otherwise

turned out—dislocated

healed—made whole or well

Second, we must remove! If you have ever been injured—broken a bone, torn a ligament, or dislocated a joint—you know that you must go through a time of rehabilitation before you can run again. This kind of therapy is protective. You need to regain your strength so you won't re-injure yourself. For example, you take every precaution to walk on flat, stable surfaces. Similarly, "make straight paths" means removing every obstacle from our course and making the running surface as straight and smooth as possible.

Q: *Nehemiah had to clear away rubble before he could rebuild the walls (Neh. 4:10). What does that situation in Jerusalem suggest to you about the importance of removing obstacles?*

_____

_____

_____

_____

_____

The author of Hebrews moves from straightening out the runner (12:12) to straightening up the racetrack (12:13) by alluding to Proverbs 4:26: "Ponder the path of thy feet, and let all thy ways be established." The command in Hebrews 12:13 is to remove every obstacle that could cause us to stumble into sin. This reminds us of the author's initial charge in the first verse of Hebrews 12 to "lay aside every weight, and the sin which doth so easily beset us." An obstacle could include any person, activity, or habit that would hinder us from successfully running the race. Renewal happens when we get up, clear the track, focus on the goal, and run the race.

Q: *Are there obstacles in your life that you have the ability to remove? Are you willing to do that? What initial steps should you take?*

_____

_____

_____

_____

_____

Pursue!

HEBREWS 12: 14
Follow peace with all men, and holiness, without which no man shall see the Lord:

WORD STUDY

follow—pursue; press toward

peace—harmony between individuals

Third, we must pursue! In order to experience spiritual renewal we must continually and passionately pursue relational harmony (peace) and spiritual and moral integrity (holiness). The Greek word translated *follow* has an interesting twist. It is also translated *persecute*. We are to pursue peace and holiness the way Paul passionately persecuted and imprisoned believers prior to his conversion (Phil. 3:6). Peter commands us to "seek peace, and ensue [pursue] it" (1 Pet. 3:11). Paul commands, "Let us therefore follow after [pursue] the things which make for peace" (Rom. 14:19).

The preferable option in any relationship is peace: "If it be possible, as much as lieth in you, live peaceably with all men." (Rom. 12:18). This includes resolving conflict and living in harmony with everyone. In other words, there is a relational component to spiritual renewal. We aren't running on the course by ourselves. And therefore, it is vitally important to be at peace with others so we can encourage each other.

Q: *In Philippians 2:1–8, what does Paul identify as crucial to Christian unity? Whose example does Paul use? What does this kind of peace have to do with spiritual renewal?*

_____

_____

_____

_____

_____

Q: *Are you living harmoniously with others? What would you need to pursue in order to develop peace and grow?*

_____

_____

_____

_____

_____

Holiness is the result of the sacrifice of Christ, by which believers have their consciences cleansed from sin and gain access into the presence of God (Heb. 10:10, 14). This holiness has to be practically worked out in our daily actions and habits:

> But as he which hath called you is holy, so be ye holy in all manner of conversation. (1 Pet. 1:15)

> For God hath not called us unto uncleanness, but unto holiness. (1 Thess. 4:7)

> But now being made free from sin, and become
> servants to God, ye have your fruit unto holiness,
> and the end everlasting life. (Rom. 6:22)

In the face of chastening, we cannot yield to the emotions of anger, discouragement, and unbelief. Rather, we must aim for the internal change of character that is produced through accepting suffering and pursuing Christlikeness—holiness. The promise to those who pursue peace and holiness is a vision of God—we will see the Lord. This culminates in glory—an eternal vision of the one who is now invisible even to us (1 Pet. 1:8–9). It also includes a consistent life of faith that sees what is not seen. We who pursue the character of God enjoy the beatific—blissfully happy—vision of God within our own hearts.

Q: *What are some of the unseen realities the writer of Hebrews was referring to in Hebrews 11:7, 8, 10, 13, 27; 12:22–24?*

_____

_____

_____

_____

_____

What is renewal? It is the quickening of the spiritual life of the believer. It evidences itself through a fresh resolve to obey God. It brings us back to running the race in the same manner as when we first began it—not only preparing ourselves but also clearing the track of obstacles. It results in holiness, a distinctive way of life that conforms to the privilegd position God has granted us in Christ.

Discussion Questions

1. *What is God's calling on your life according to 1 Thessalonians 4:7? Is He using discipline in your life right now? Based on this study, how should you respond?*

_____

_____

_____

_____

_____

2. *It's hard when you are feeling weak and weary to strengthen yourself to resolve, remove, and pursue. Based on the exhortations in Hebrews 3:13 and 10:25, how will you be able to follow the commands of 12:12–14?*

_____

_____

_____

_____

_____

8

Final Warnings

HEBREWS 12:15-17

Looking diligently lest any man fail of the grace of God; lest any root of bitterness springing up trouble you, and thereby many be defiled; Lest there be any fornicator, or profane person, as Esau, who for one morsel of meat sold his birthright. For ye know how that afterward, when he would have inherited the blessing, he was rejected: for he found no place of repentance, though he sought it carefully with tears.

This section of Hebrews concludes with a charge to the entire church. We are urged to carefully watch over the spiritual state of other believers by "looking diligently." This is the mutual responsibility of all of us to support and to guard each other from falling away from the Faith. No one is running solo in the Christian race. Hebrews is filled with exhortations to believers to protect one another. The passage began with "a cloud of witnesses" who ran before us (Heb. 12:1). It climaxes with our responsibilities to those running alongside us.

> But exhort one another daily, while it is called To day; lest any of you be hardened through the deceitfulness of sin. (Heb. 3:13)

> Let us therefore fear, lest, a promise being left us of entering into his rest, any of you should seem to come short of it. (Heb. 4:1)

> Let us labour therefore to enter into that rest, lest any man fall after the same example of unbelief. (Heb. 4:11)

Not forsaking the assembling of ourselves together, as the manner of some is; but exhorting
one another: and so much the more, as ye see the
day approaching. (Heb. 10:25)

Q: *How often are we to exhort one another? Why does the author emphasize accountability? What should this kind of mutual edification look like?*

_____

_____

_____

_____

Q: *What kind of "rest" was the writer talking about in Hebrews 4?*

_____

_____

_____

_____

Q: *What does Hebrews 10:25 say about assembling as a church? Why is this important?*

_____

_____

_____

_____

HEBREWS 12:15

Looking diligently lest any man fail of the grace of God; . . .

WORD STUDY

looking diligently—seeing to something, overseeing, taking care of; looking upon

lest—or else; otherwise

fail—to lack; to be late; to postpone; to come late, be behind, come short

grace—unmerited kindness

The author has already exhorted the discouraged to get back into the race with three direct commands, which we summarized in the previous lesson as *resolve, remove,* and *pursue.*

Q: *Review the three commands in Hebrews 12:12–14 by writing them out.*

_____

_____

_____

_____

_____

Now, he concludes by charging the church to guard against potential apostasy with three strong warnings—"looking diligently lest . . . lest . . . lest." In other words, the church must corporately see to it that everyone finishes the race. Otherwise, some of those who are running alongside us will suffer serious consequences.

Warning #1—See to It That No One Misses Out on God's Grace!

The image in this phrase involves a group of runners where everyone is being urged to keep up the pace and stay with the others. However, as time goes on some runners may begin to lag behind. Going a little more slowly is one thing, but some may drop out of the race altogether.

Q: *What's slowing you down spiritually? What other temptations can hinder you from keeping up the pace or even from staying in the race?*

_____

_____

_____

_____

_____

So we must care for one another—"Looking diligently lest any man fail of the grace of God" (12:15). In other words, see to it that no one comes short of obtaining grace. We need to continually encourage each other to faithfully finish the race. We must persevere to the end! We also need to recognize that God's grace that gets us into the race is the same grace that enables us to finish the race. The writer's point is that professing believers who fall short of finishing the race will miss eternal life in God's presence. This warning echoes an earlier passage:

> Let us therefore fear, lest, a promise being left us of entering into his rest, any of you should seem to come short of it. For unto us was the gospel preached, as well as unto them: but the word preached did not profit them, not being mixed with faith in them that heard it. (Heb. 4:1–2)

There were many Israelites who left Egypt during the Exodus but who never entered the land of Canaan. They missed the Promised Land because they hardened their hearts in unbelief.

> And to whom sware he that they should not enter into his rest, but to them that believed not? So we see that they could not enter in because of unbelief. (Heb. 3:18–19)

Q: *What had those who weren't allowed to enter failed to believe?*

_____

_____

_____

_____

_____

However, the author assures us that if we are genuinely converted we will enjoy eternal rest with God forever.

> For we which have believed do enter into rest, as he said, As I have sworn in my wrath, if they shall enter into my rest . . . (Heb. 4:3)

The warning is clear: Don't miss grace!

> See that ye refuse not him that speaketh. For if they escaped not who refused him that spake on earth, much more shall not we escape, if we turn away from him that speaketh from heaven. (Heb. 12:25)

As we have noted previously, the point of such warnings is not to make us doubt our salvation. Those God has given eternal life to are safe and cannot perish (John 10:28). Instead, these warnings are one of God's ways of protecting us and urging us to keep looking to Jesus Christ. Sometimes we struggle to believe, but giving up is never the answer. We must keep on running, as did "the author and finisher of our faith" (Heb. 12:2).

Q: *Why would God graciously act on behalf of Israel, or on behalf of professing believers today, but then give a warning not to fall away?*

_____

_____

_____

_____

_____

Warning #2—See to It That No One Defiles Others Through His Bitterness!

HEBREWS 12:15

... lest any root of bitterness springing up trouble
you, and thereby many be defiled; ...

WORD STUDY

bitterness—derived from an adjective meaning sharp
(like a tent stake), acrid (like the taste of poison), or harsh
and virulent (in attitude or behavior)

springing up—bringing forth, producing; growing, coming up

trouble—to crowd in; to annoy; to cause trouble

defiled—stained; polluted

Those who miss this grace of God can potentially become
contaminants within the church. The roots of bitterness mentioned in 12:15 are not primarily situations but people. This
phrase is an allusion to Deuteronomy 29:18: "Lest there should
be among you man, or woman, or family, or tribe, whose heart
turneth away this day from the Lord our God, to go and serve
the gods of these nations; lest there should be among you a root
that beareth gall and wormwood." Moses warned about the

noxious influence of those in his wilderness congregation who had turned away from following the Lord to worshiping idols.

So, this "root of bitterness" consists of people who because of hardships and suffering have become bitter and rebellious against God and have dropped out of the race. These people can cause great damage to the church because of their controlling ("trouble you") and contaminating ("many be defiled") influence.

Q: *Have you experienced or observed any community of believers (e.g., family, church, school) that has been polluted by bitterness? Write down a couple of truths from Hebrews 12 that would preserve such communities from defilement.*

_____

_____

_____

_____

_____

Historically, such people have been called *apostates*—defectors from the Faith. You may wonder whether these individuals are actually saved. There is general agreement that apostates were never believers in the first place. Their influence troubles the body of Christ and is very contagious. We have an obligation to keep watch over each other because unholy responses to trials quickly pollute the body of Christ and lead to unbelief.

Q: *What trials have tempted you to grow into a "root of bitterness"? How did God help you overcome these temptations?*

_____

_____

_____

_____

_____

Q: *How were you helped through the mutual edification of other believers? What could you do to help others in* similar situations?

_____

_____

_____

_____

_____

Warning #3—See to It That No One Forfeits His Soul to Lust and Idolatry!

HEBREWS 12:16–17

Lest there be any fornicator, or profane person, as Esau, who for one morsel of meat sold his birthright. For ye know how that afterward, when he would have inherited the blessing, he was rejected: for he found no place of repentance, though he sought it carefully with tears.

WORD STUDY

fornicator—a sexually immoral person

profane person—someone who despised sacred things and was therefore not permitted to join in temple worship; by implication a wicked, ungodly person

meat—food or a meal

sold—gave away; paid off

birthright—the privileges or advantages of the firstborn

would have inherited—wanted to receive or take from a predecessor

blessing—(literally, speaking well) a father's words of encouragement in conveying the inheritance to his son

place—an opportunity, room

repentance—a reversal of [his father's] decision

sought—craved, demanded

The author gives us an example of someone who missed the grace of God and became a negative influence—Esau, the firstborn son of Isaac. He is condemned as a *fornicator* (sexually immoral man). Though the Old Testament never describes him in that manner (Genesis 26:34–35), tradition paints Esau as a lustful man. He was also *profane*, meaning his pursuits in life were without God. He had no spiritual desires and fed only his physical, sensual appetites. Because of his enslavement to lust, he had virtually no concern about his spiritual privileges and opportunities as the firstborn son of Isaac.

Q: *Consider the connections between Hebrews 12:10–11 and 12:16. Why do you think the Holy Spirit guided the author to use the example of a sexually immoral, profane person?*

_____

_____

_____

_____

_____

Think about Esau's place in redemptive history. By birthright he was heir to the sacred blessings of the Abrahamic Covenant. Though this included material prosperity, it primarily involved a spiritual heritage. Esau was in the family line of God's blessings on the world through the coming Messiah and His gospel. However, these privileges required a consistent life of faith in the present even though their primary fulfillment was far in the future. When put to the test, Esau sold his birthright for a single meal to satisfy a temporary desire (Gen. 25:27–34), rather than fixing his hope on what God had promised.

Q: *What God-given privileges are you tempted to take for granted? What is necessary to be ready to overcome such temptations?*

_____

_____

_____

_____

_____

Kent Hughes describes Esau's failure this way:

> Esau grew up a big, hairy, red-headed lout whose focus was fun (hunting), food, and females. Big "Red" (for that is what his nickname "Edom" meant) came in from the field hungry after hunting and found Jacob cooking some lentile stew. So he motioned, "Quick, let me have some of that red stew! I'm famished!", to which Jacob made the incredible proposition, "First sell me your birthright", only to be followed by the even more incredible flip response, "Look, I am about to die.... What good is the birthright to me?" Unbelievable! Old sweaty Red chose a cheap meal over the divine promise.[1]

---

[1] R. Kent Hughes, *Hebrews: An Anchor for the Soul* (Wheaton: Crossway, 1993), 2:184.

Esau treated his privileges as negligible and insignificant. He later regretted his decision, but it was too late to change it. The decision was irrevocable! No amount of tears could undo it. He had failed the test, and this failure revealed the true nature of his heart. God intends these words to warn those who are in the position of turning away from Him and His promises. Sadly, some make irrevocable choices with eternal consequences.

Q: *What did Esau search for diligently—repentance or the blessing? Why didn't God give him a second chance? (Hint: The answer to the first question is critical to answering the second.)*

Q: *Read 2 Corinthians 7:9–10. How does Paul contrast godly sorrow and worldly sorrow? Can you think of an example in your life or someone else's when sorrow amounted to worldly regret?*

It doesn't matter if we're tempted by sex or money or the desire to control other people or whatever; our flesh naturally extinguishes joy in the Creator so that we seek happiness only in

His creation. This twisted desire makes God seem totally unreal to us. What we physically sense becomes the only reality. In reality, what we are experiencing is not the pull of creation but the deceitfulness of sin. We lose our ability to discern and make wise decisions and keep coming back to the questions "Is this really wrong of me to want this? Don't I deserve this pleasure?" Such wrong thinking crops up, not only where Jesus is not named, but also when professing believers despise their sacred privileges. So the challenge to the church is to keep running by laying aside distractions, fighting sin to the death, and looking to Jesus Christ. God is at work disciplining us for holiness, and He has given us the mutual responsibility of helping each other realize this divine prize. Heed His warnings. Believe His promises. And run all the way to glory!

Discussion Questions

1. *In Hebrews 12:15 Paul uses the expression to "fail of the grace of God"? What is his parallel expression in Galatians 2:21? What does this look like in real life?*

2. *In light of the second and third warnings on pages 75 and 77, what kinds of sins should we be especially on guard against in the church?*

_____

_____

3. *Does Galatians 6:1–5 apply to encouraging each other to run the race? If so, how?*

_____

_____

_____

_____

_____